THE HEART IS AN ATTIC

Srividya Sivakumar

Hawakal Publishers

Published by Hawakal Publishers, 185 Kali Temple Road,
Nimta, Kolkata 700049

Email: info@hawakal.com

Website: www.hawakal.com

First edition (India): April, 2018
Copyright © Srividya Sivakumar 2018
Cover designed by Chitrangi
Author photograph: Shantini S Diaz

ISBN: 978-93-87883-03-1 (Paperback)

Price: INR 300.00 | USD 9.99

To Krishna. For being my always.

FOREWORD

In this, Srividya's second collection, we are invited—as houseguests are—to spend a few hours in the intimacy of a writer's home. It begins as all visits do. We sit laughing in her living room, reassuring ourselves that we are no demon guests ("Guests"). After a while, we wonder whether she has a Virginia Woolfesque room of her own (the answer is no, she sits down to write everywhere in her apartment). Ever the provocateur, this host then gently nudges us to wander towards that most mysterious and unsettling of all rooms in her home (and our lives): the attic.

The attic! This darkly brooding, unkempt little room *is* the antechamber of the heart. It resides in each of us: the only custodian of our truest (but oft-hidden) self. Packed with old suitcases full of half-forgotten, but not yet abandoned, loves, desires and grievances; the attic is our confessional. And Srividya its confessor, in this collection, *The Heart is an Attic*.

In this second offering, she continues in the tradition of *The Blue Note* and remains the poet of the "grief bludgeoned" human heart. Without doubt, she is principally a poet of the female experience. Hers are songs of the professional, urban Everywoman, who juggles the competing demands of love, work, home *and* of society ("Do Fiery Feminists Fall In Love?,"

"Eggs," "Facade," "Merry Widow," and "Mother Knows Best.")

Srividya is the poet of Everywoman's inner romantic life and of her unabashed female sexuality. With her trademark searing honesty, she writes of "*being a woman and knowing a man*" ("Stealth"). We meet the woman who confidently owns the "*room between my legs*" ("Wormhole") and its happy adventures: "*Three four five – I have stopped keeping score/Bed to bed is a journey*" ("One-Night Stand").

She investigates the complex nature of the companionship that exists between a man and a woman. This leitmotif dominates Srividya's writing. In *The Heart is an Attic* beloveds oscillate wildly between ambiguity and certainty:

> *Love is a tchotchke. Like a pack of batteries or gum at the checkout counter in a wily supermarket. Picked up on a whim.*
>
> *...Except when it's not significant. Then love is the red and gold table. It's the opium in your peace pipe. It's the matryoshka doll that keeps unravelling.*

And

> *We work best in ambiguity.*

There is the continual waiting. In the pages that follow, we immediately recognise the "*woman who waits*," the "*almost bride*" and the stench of power play between "*the one left*" and "*the one to leave*." There is loneliness; at times, even lovers are "*too much for your solitude*" ("Hiraeth")—mere intruders in the attic-heart. Why, there is even torture: "*Sometimes love holds your head under water. Not hard, just firm*" ("Waterboarding").

Hers is an unflinching dissection of the many moods of love: mundane, just-a-little-careless, wishing-for-more, pungent. In her hands, the topic of 'love' turns matryoshka doll, keeps unravelling. Yes, there is every shade of disillusionment in these poems, as Srividya turns into the poet of lost love stories, quite literally in "Declivity."

Even so, a semblance of certainty does rear its reassuring head in comfortable old loves, who do sometimes actually win against thrilling new ones:

> *Old love is a pair of thick socks, an old t-shirt, a worn at the seat and knees corduroy that clings and comforts.*
>
> *New love has dropped the napkin on the floor and is oblivious.*
>
> *Old love is writing this poem.*

The "*old love*" or the "*the almost bride*" who inhabit this collection are often women with both creative jobs and homes to run. This Everywoman "*is*

7

holding a pen/ is frantically cleaning the house" ("Stonewall"). In *The Heart is an Attic*, Srividya becomes an unparalleled rapporteur of the nature of the creative life. Here the artist is also lover, partner, wife, homemaker and daughter-in-law:

> and there are things to be done
> as far as the eye can see
> even poets lead mundane lives
> they are hosts, they are wives
> there are demands on made on their time
> and there are people waiting
> but not in line

Srividya fearlessly examines the prose of domestic life for the woman of the house, who "*cooks his breakfast...scrubs the toilet bowls...bakes the birthday cake, wakes up early, goes to sleep late*" ("Every Day's a Celebration"). Even on the day she is feted for professional success ("Aftermath 1") or when her debutant poem dies at the hands of its first readers ("Obituary"), the poet-wife must put away her heart and carry on. It is business-as-usual: "*two loads of laundry await*" and "*there are vessels that need putting away*" ("Aftermath 1").

The world that Everywoman inhabits is one where both lovers and audiences seem to roam freely with knives. This is also the indifferent world of child labour, caste discrimination, violence against women and very little civic responsibility ("Every Day's a

Celebration," "Jisha," "Magic Lamp"). Nonetheless, it is in this highly ambiguous and very uncertain world—*"a world that demands more than I can give"* ("Haunting in Coimbatore") that we must all work and play. Where then should we look for the courage to carry on? I found comfort in a beautiful lesson about human nature that I discovered in this outstanding collection of poetry: that there is some measure of redemption in art. Because our fragile, yearning and easily disappointed human heart is willing to accept in art, the ambiguity it so staunchly resists in life. Read these poems. Let them speak to you. And then let it be.

Anupama Sekhar
Director, Culture
Asia-Europe Foundation, Singapore

INTRODUCTION

A lot has happened in the six years since the publication of my first book of poems. *The Blue Note* opened up doors, allowing me to be a TEDx speaker, not once but twice, allowing me to read my work at literary events and celebrations of poetry.

Along the way, I had the unimaginable opportunity to write a weekly column on poetry for *The Hindu* for eighteen months. The column, "Running on Poetry," let me delve even further into this world that I am fortunate to inhabit. More importantly, it taught me how kind and generous poetry practitioners can be. Writing to poets I have long admired and hearing back from them with nothing but gentle encouragement and appreciation is a magnificent thrill that cannot really be described.

But the second time of publishing a book has been hard for me.

There is a weight of expectation—my own—and a self-consciousness to not make a fool of myself. Being hypercritical about my poetry does not help either. Being turned down by publishers, and advised to get a "poetry editor," (a new term for me) was also crushing. I put away the manuscript. I continued to write poetry.

And then I reminded myself that I'd been writing long before I had an audience, and decades before I had been first published.

That the reason I write in the first place is for myself and my need to speak—often unutterable—thoughts and feelings. *The Heart is an Attic* is a result of that soul-searching.

Srividya Sivakumar
March, 2018
Coimbatore

ACKNOWLEDGEMENTS

"Impressionist," "Pamuk Plays the Palanguzhi," have appeared in *Noble/Gas Qtrly*. "Sunder," has been featured in the *40 Under 40* anthology. Heartfelt thanks to the editors and publishers.

The heart, *my* heart, is an attic. And the light shines through because of the people on this page.

When a poet you've long respected is (as always) generous with her time and her words, it creates a joy and assurance that is irrepressible. Arundhathi Subramaniam, for your grace and kindness, thank you.

Anupama Sekhar, oldest friend and keeper of my conscience. Thank you for the Foreword. Your insight, humour and eloquence are delightful and enrich the book so, so much.

To everyone at Hawakal. Thank you for your faith, time and attention to detail.

To Shan, sister and super-efficiency engine. For your cross-referencing skills and for the wise (and often exasperated) counsel, thank you.

To Linda Ashok. For the brainstorming, conversations and feedback, thank you.

Thank you to my family for the help, care and encouragement.

To Poornima, from, 'oh wow,' to 'what the hell,' your reactions to my poems tell me whatever I need to know. Thank you for your (brutal) candour, and (hysterical fits) friendship.

To Vimo. My friend of almost three decades. Having a personal cheerleader is a constant, thanks to you.

Thank you to my friend, Cynthia. For the pep talks and the suggestions.

To Sooraj. For email assistance, unstoppable cheer and support, and some truly terrible jokes. Thank you.

Finally, to Krishna. My partner. My safe place. My strength.

CONTENTS

EGGS

even the most *hard-boiled* man

fried in the heat of a no-frills space

filled with memories and promises of babies

who need to be *coddled*

is *scrambled* like a well-made breakfast.

his wife is cooking for them a delicious

worrisome *omelette*

that's been *basted* in an impersonal i- can't- be-

bothered

industrial steel kitchen

full of *poached* dreams and aspirations

and *devilled* by an addled brain.

unwilling children are *smoked* out by the tantalizing

promise

of life always being a *sunny side up* experience.

baked into all this are expectations

of familial duty and requirements for lineage.

the man is merely *soft-boiled*

his role not as essential as the woman's

he is a supplier at best

17

but if not him

any tom, bansi or *benedict* would do.

as long as the supply hits the *bull's eye*

how does it matter who's doing the giving ?

shirred into submission

pickled into passivity

scalloped by sacred texts

bodies now obey not each other's rhythms

but that of society's.

scotch helps

sex obviously has not.

eggs, anyone?

(RMU- Reproductive Medicine Unit)

BROMIDIC

i talk about you like you are still in my life.
Like you're walking along in the morning and you
cross my house and when you see me in the garden
being a poet, you ask me for a cup of black coffee.
Like you're swimming against a placid river and spy
me sitting on a water-drenched rock, drying off from
a spin in a whirlpool, and you ask me how to broil a
fish.
Like you're at an old books store and are sneezing
because of the vanillin and see me deeply inhale from
a book about Judas, and ask me for a
recommendation.
Like you're signing off on some important papers
and i am sitting at the other end of the table,
scribbling away and you ask me for a few words you
can use.
Like you're harvesting paddy in your fields, calf- deep
in water, brushing past iridescent snakes, and you see
me trying hard to stay on the not enough pathway
and ask me for a palmyra fan.

Like you're waiting at a traffic signal, annoyed as always, and notice me next to you, waving to get your attention, and you ask me where i am going to.

Like you're in my house, stalking about, draped on the sofa, looking at me walking away, and you ask me for some more sugar.

Yes, i speak about you like we talk every day. Like we meet every day.

Like we are in love every day.

Little do they know that it's been a long while, and that i am slowly forgetting the touch of your hand and the look in your eyes.

CONSTRUCTION

Stripped of its frills and trims and knobs and colours
It showed itself for what it is.
Some child labour brick and some muddy water
cement.
It is a buildi, not even a building, unadorned and
unloved.
It showed itself to be plain. A house.
What can make it a home? To sparkle brighter than
the hideous green that crowds it.
It waits for her hopeful heart.
And his leaving legs.

LONG DISTANCE

we work best in small measures and measured time

in rare appearances and hesitant smiles

we work best in the afternoon light

and as the voices of the night

we work best without the chains

of demands and complaints

without the guise of normalcy

we get to be you and me

we work best in ambiguity

in this deep desire that should bind but sets us free

we work because of the miles that separate your life

your bed and mine.

yes we work in fractured splintered days

and interminable hours

in words of passion and opinion

and in the same stars

we work in intent and promise

even if they aren't to be

we work in the only way we can

we work as you and me.

EVERY DAY'S A CELEBRATION

"Happy Women's Day," he says to her as she cooks his breakfast, packs his lunch, picks up the groceries, cuts the vegetables, does the laundry, folds the clothes, puts them away, helps with homework, helps with medicines, calls the plumber, calls the carpenter, cleans the bathrooms, scrubs the toilet bowls, dusts the house, waters the plants, makes the casserole, bakes the birthday cake, wakes up early, goes to sleep late.

"Happy Women's Day," he says to her as she breaks stones, carries loads on her head, on her back, on her shoulders, in her heart. Coughs over an open fire, waits for the dark, to take a bath, to piss, to shit, to change her blood-soaked rag. Bears another child whom she will not know, bears her man grunting and burrowing into her, bears the slaps and words and looks and taunts.

But yes, Happy Women's Day.

STONEWALL

Arms that only know how to hold (you)

have to learn to fold

themselves to the side of my body

Tucked between sheets

and under pillows

Anywhere but around you

A hand that held palms and fingers

that soothed an aching head back knee or ankle

with a sure (and vested) touch

Now is held against my face

is holding a pen

is frantically cleaning the house

It doesn't know what to do when it's not polishing

your skin to a warm brown.

Legs that wrapped themselves around one leg or two

Around a waist

Over a shoulder

Against a back

Now stretch as far as they can go

and they go nowhere important.

Yes. This body needs to learn to rearrange itself.

These eyes have to find some other place; not your
face
These lips need to give up their dependence on lips
and fingers and chest and brow
The tongue needs a new language because it speaks
only of your gentle touch and awkwardness
Every part of me feels withdrawn parched and bereft
Of every part of you
But i need to win this battle
Otherwise you'll continue to kiss close-mouthed
Turn away from my reaching out hands
Move me away when i get closer
Run. Shrink. And make a quick escape
Rejection is hard but rebuilding is more so
But i am starting with rebuilding
i am starting with me.

LENT

i met you on a contemplative Christmas.

The snowflakes sizzled as they landed on your shoulders.

You emerged from a fog-filled forest lit up by fairy lights and lanterns low on branches.

You were the gift, i decided. My prayers had been answered. My letter received.

Through saints and sainthood, catechism and community, we had communion. We conversed from words to hearts. The hard pews were a stern lectern and the ocean kept trying to see in.

What was the magic we wove in the naves? We knelt down, love slaves. And asked for a miracle a moment a memory. To want and have at the same time, if it could be.

Love was stained-glass gorgeous. Your hair was blue my body was burnt orange. Our sighs were matins and mass.

But the nails weren't too far away. The thorns were there for us to ignore. And the singing was soon off-

key. And the pews were painted black. All the
colours fled, swept away by anger and regret.
i gave you up for Lent, i said.
i meant for life.

CONGÉ

You've left and left me with memories

what do i do with these?

take them with you

won't you please,

so i may go and live again.

here is the sun-drenched day

where we kissed in the shadow-filled way

and here are the flowers we crushed

under us as we plucked

love from the time we had

now that memory makes me sad

so take this with you

that moonlit ride

you and me, your almost bride

the meadow was an eerie shade

eager was the love we made

and take this warmth from my hand

that held yours as we slept

and take this soul that waited so long

and this secret that it has kept

take the wine, take the food

take the chocolate, take the soup
take the fruit, take the bread
take your presence from my head
love take your love away
let me not miss it not a single day
take all this you've left with you
but please don't forget
take me too.

Congé: An unceremonious dismissal or rejection of someone.

AFTERMATH 1

i'm in the paper

a poet in the news

for once being feted and not abused

i smile at the buzz that surrounds me

i am amused

i am bemused

i've enjoyed my time in the sun

this was easy

compared to the battles i've won

everyone seems happy

well i hope they are

and ever if they weren't

i'm the happiest by far

but right now two loads of laundry await

ready to greet their washing cycle fate

and there are vessels that need putting away

and a home crying out for some attention

so i remove my poet garb

lay down my wand, my trusted old pen

unpin the celebrated cape from me

and sit

calmly

count to ten

breakfast awaits

even if it's only toast

my crown can wait

it'll be tarnished at the most

the paper's folded away

in a corner of my memory

and there are things to be done

as far as the eyes can see

even poets lead mundane lives

they are hosts, they are wives

there are demands made on their time

and there are people waiting

but not in line.

FAÇADE

Invisible breasts

Hiding behind *hijab*s

Held unforgiven by underwired demicups

Stuffed into silk satin corsets

Disciplined by high-back blouses

Limited by camisoles

Fettered by 'free the nipple' t-shirts

Swaying in the inbuilt bra and string them up *choli*s

Invisible breasts

Hidden behind a lover's mouth

Clutched as life by a man's fingers

Bound by leather in a mask

Clamped by clips and kisses

Invisible breasts

Blue green veins under the skin

Cigarette ash on the curve

Underboob tattoos for the win

Blood milk as is deserved

Invisible breasts

But not ignored

Stared at

Leered

Pinched and groped

Sucked on

Suckled

Held together tight

Slept on as though a right.

Invisible breasts

But not really.

Visible invisible breasts.

CLASSROOM

I see reproach in eyes that want to ask but don't—why this? And I want to ask but don't—why not? I can swear in three languages, of which one of them is this. I can cut up trees for expensive sheets and say my piece in bits. I count in my head. Moan in bed. Sing with ease. Play at striptease with it guiding me through. Yes, you in the last row with your bull tattoo and *jallikattu* views. Am I less Tamil for speaking my mind and more than my mother tongue? Or, you whose demure downcast eyes look at a blue screen with a boy's name on it. Shall I apologise for the breath of my ambition to patronise this one space I can call home?

Or you from a fish state who says you do not read in it because it was used to colonise. Give up cricket. And the railways. And the post. What? Hard to do? What do we really know about how we communicate? If you have nothing to say, no words will ever be adequate. If you do, haven't you said it already?

TCHOTCHKE

Love is a tchotchke.

Like a pack of batteries or gum at the checkout counter in a wily supermarket. Picked up on a whim. Some say in $1/5^{th}$ of a second. That unthought out. Once home, you put the batteries in an overfilled table draw. You'll look for it weeks later by which time you'd have forgotten where you left it. You make your way through the gum a lazy Sunday jamming with friends and swigging cider. The tastes mingle in your mouth and it's unpleasant. You persevere. And sure enough, you like it now. You enter love with the same carelessness. A ruthlessness in fate, a riding on the coattails of luck good and bad. It's as insignificant as the rescued wrapping paper, the old bunch of flowers, the variegated satin ribbons that clutter that table draw. Except when it's not insignificant. Then love is the red and gold table. It's the opium in your peace pipe. It's the matryoshka doll that keeps unravelling.

But the entrance into this world of mixed tastes and deep heartbreak, is often, almost always, a quick trolley ride down an aisle full of mines.

Tchotchke: A small object that is decorative rather than strictly functional; a trinket.

JISHA

Didn't your flesh crawl ?
she is dalit after all
and we share nothing with them
not tumblers daughters or village walls.
your cock should have shrivelled and died
the thought of it inside
a spinster a law student a low caste woman
living on the street and hence proven
that she was up to no good at all.
and yet here you are
helping yourself to her self
like you were some coveted guest
helping yourself to her life- bringing cunt
her skin
her organs
her mind.
was she blind to try and move beyond
a strictly laid out life plan and rule?
and so here you are.
her knight in shining armour
to teach her her place

buried in the ground and in the inner pages of a
newspaper.

three minutes of sound bites and countless candle
marches later

we give her her name.

Like Jisha didn't always have one.

Afterword

Mince your words he says. Use something different. Not
cunt. Not cock. I wonder what those men called it. Did
they say her vagina is like petals? Like a beautiful delicate
rose. The way my lover says it. Did they say look at her
skin. It glitters and shines with hard work and hunger.
Touch it and see if it sticks. Did they say her breasts are
shapely. That they are golden brown and full. What did
they say? Did they say let us treat her with respect.
Delicately gently like she should be, any woman should
be. Respectfully. They did not. They were deeply human.
They are depraved bastards. With penises as small as peas.
There. Different words.

IMPRESSIONIST

A Jackson Pollock painting walks into the diner. It's
jarring in its chaos and comforting
in its method. Senses slowly drip into sharp focus
like an overloaded coffeemaker with
cheap green beans and no palm civet in sight.
The eggs are surrealistic and beg the adornment of
art and artefact. The plate is chipped
and dipped in olive oil from sustainable farms in the
east.
It's all an act of persuasion to belie fears and soothe
jittery nerves shot up with too
much strong coffee and no sugar.
Give me a kiss, he tells her.
She removes her eyeteeth and her lips are unicorn
breath.
Let's touch so my colours bleed into you and your
spices mix into me.
A painting walks out. A Modigliani nude, it hangs
askew in a brown study.

WATERBOARDING

Sometimes love holds your head under water. Not hard, just firm. Hand on your skull, a sure grip, to make sure you don't get any ideas. Empty your mind. Surrender to the water. You're going nowhere and you're not getting out of here. Sometimes love takes a knife to your throat and moves it along your neck, between your breasts to your arm and your wrist. It presses in on that throbbing nerve and draws tears. Allow love to tear into your skin. It's in your blood anyway and now you can see it stain your path to another world. Sometimes love lays you on a flower carpet so thick and so bright that you tread light-footed, unwilling to stir up the harmony until you, prone, breathe in and out and feel the thorns enter you. Thorns are wounds and fit right in with this version of love. Breathe in song breathe out betrayal and watch the shadows glisten. Sometimes love is a backstabbing friend. Sometimes it's a selfish child at the teat. Sometimes it's a slap in the face, a kick to the floor, a possession that's brutal and single-minded. Sometimes love is a third-degree technique and it takes no prisoners.

OBITUARY

a poem died tonight

in love and despite

the struggles of the writer and me

it withered it gave up it perished endlessly.

so final is its death

i remarked on its beauty and said

oh we should all die in this way

as a poet a lover in eternal disgrace.

this poem was written with much thought

with passion and words shop-soiled and bought

but when it came time to share it with you

you looked askance and i knew

my poem was breathing its last

it would be done

and it would be fast.

my poem it died tonight

i loved it

i put up a good fight

but it's done now

my poem has sunk without a trace

except in the despair that marks my face.

VELLUM

speak into my skin.

in the language you call home.

fish fragrant   wishing well deep

      rice starched

cat love   cricket chirping

      catechism calling

paddy fields lush   waterfall laden   brandy

soaked long legged

broad chested   pianist fingers

      articulate mind walking

space gazing devoted love making time man

beautiful.

BYSTANDER

You'd use your tongue
and drink tears from my eyes
today when i cry,
the canned laughter of the unfunny comedy
mocks my desperation
and you look on steadily at the screen
wondering what to do with a wife
high on hormones
and pregnant with thousands of dead babies.
or you with your smooth smile and dancer's eyes
would call and visit and tell me it will be fine
now you conduct panel discussions
and my tears are a wall of silence and reproach.

ORCHESTRATED

Your body is music and poetry. I can play a song on your ribs. And sing against your lips.

I can touch your smooth skin. And breathe your chest in.

I can span your waist. And keep pace. With your legs and their length. With your fingers and their scent.

Your body was made for me. It was made for my eternity.

Its shoulders carry a secret tune.

Its arms carry my heart and me.

STEALTH

You left so completely so convincingly that for a while there i didn't even know. Your t-shirt kept me warm at night, the bed still fragrant from your perfume, my fingers immersed in the heat of your skin. One should leave as quietly as completely as you do. It's an art and not an easy one to master. Like poetry and appreciating single malts.

In the days weeks months to come, i wandered about haunted by a movie in translation, warm welcoming shoulders and coffee in the rain. An empty bottle of wine kept me company as did the remembrance of a voice on the phone line. i would say more, but there's a chance that you might be reading this in some distant land in a disparate time zone and recognise yourself in this yearning. No more feeling off-balance. No more quickening of heartbeat. No more awareness of being a woman and knowing a man. As the silence grew i knew or tried to that this was done if it had ever begun. And that i was the page turned over. The friend of circumstances. The woman who waits.

It's not painful. Now. Or hurtful. It's life i guess and I've given it a mouthful. Taken deep breaths of the loneliness that you left behind and then made peace with it. i am not bereft. Nor filled with longing or bewildered at my change of fortunes.

It was written in the stars and in the runes that i would be the one left and not the one to leave.

GUESTS

any day now

the demons will come home

chasing me through the forest

knocking at my door

and i will welcome them

they'll make themselves at home

stretching out on the sofa

curling up on the floor

they'll drink water from the refrigerator

snack on chocolate from the biscuit tin

they'll pluck my precious hibiscus

and call themselves my kin.

neighbours won't see them

lolling on my bookshelf

they'll look at me and wonder (as always)

about the world in which i dwell

but the demons they see me

they know that i know they're there

i do not repel them

quite the opposite in fact

they wear colours of my disappointments

the fabric of my failed romance

they smile the smile of knowing

knowing they will always care

the demons have come knocking

and i have willingly let them in

slowly they take over my day my life

all together now, *sin*.

EXEGESIS

Between us my love, there is no distance.

There is an ocean of unsaid truths and uttered lies.

Waves of bobbing babies and indifferent biological

necessity sex.

But there is no distance.

There are all the misunderstandings and the long

unending interminable logic-defying silences.

There are one line utterances and monosyllabic

conversations.

There is the deep pit of stubbornness and the

relentlessness of unrelenting.

There is your ego and my pride.

Your apathy and my ignorance.

There is your work and my life.

There is your love. And my version of it.

But no, there is no distance.

MAGIC LAMP

the devotee is dressed in black like me

perhaps that's why he turns to take a leisurely look at

us

we walk past but his eyes bore holes that make our

clothes seem to flee

each day the devotee stops and prays

his devotion to god does not extend to the road

that carries his refuse and his hogwash

the devotee smokes. god looks after his lungs.

he drinks. god looks after his liver.

he stares. god gives him good intentions and noble

thoughts.

The devotee doesn't pick up his garbage. god sends

him a national cleanliness campaign.

WORMHOLE

because of the distance between us

i finally see how much my body can hold

and the heart. the head. the eyes

i can cross continents in two strides

take the world in with all its good byes

i can hold a man a thought a child

i can fill my heart for a long passionate while

yes so much space has been freed up

without you i feel feather-light

it must be your departure that's making my skin glow

friends wonder but what do they know

my head multiplies complex numbers

okay no it doesn't but who'd want to

my head is filled with thoughts of someone else

it's not overwhelming or overpowering

i can safely dwell here in this space

that smells like almonds and feels like water

it's hot now. he's doing that to me

and yet there's room

between my legs

beneath the sheets

balanced on the tips of my nipples

and the soles of my feet

i can crumble discontent like it is smoked weed and

spit you out, an afterthought

lord knows that's what i did.

IRONIC

ruthless,

you do not text or call

or make any move to drive a distance

to come see me

while i walk though meadows that we've planted

together

and swim in waters we made love in

and draw patterns on the sands

that heard our conversations.

yes things change

oh how they change

me in my silence and you in your facile guilt

make for an estrangement

that is peculiar

and almost funny

if it weren't so damn sad.

MERRY WIDOW

Sometimes i'm filled with so much rage, i don't want to read but burn this unhelpful page and hurl the heavy ashes at his ugly face and turn to putrid garbage to avoid his embrace. It would take so little to stuff a pillow to that face, it would take a bit of strength to sink a knife into that rib cage, maybe slip in some poison into that drink he likes so much, but all i do is slam this damn door shut. The hapless housewife often feels rage such burning anger, seeing a fat husband and spoilt children arguing about dinner. How nice it would be to upturn this tureen of hot broth. It would have to be him- the baby's wearing a new frock. Oh my the poet! How scandalous her thoughts. Better she be boycotted, she's insane or has been bought by the devil. She's made love to him, you know, for writing this way is inhuman and has only one cure. Death to the writer! Death to the muse! Death to the pen! Death there's no excuse! Now let's go back to our pots and pans and talk of our televisions and our shopping plans, while our husbands are indifferent and our children, undisciplined. We'll cook and clean and plot and preen and put away our hearts and not vent our spleens. Thank god the poet's dead, we can breathe easy today. Wait. What's that?

Someone's walking on our grave.

HAUNTING IN COIMBATORE

how many more new years without you, my love.

how many more Christmases and Eids.

people scurry about on the streets

knowing that when they go home

they will meet their love their life

and i

go by our summer haunts

the olive fields and the fish pond

and remember toes half moss half green

and a man's bare unshamed stare.

yes it's all there

in the brass memory chest in my mind

along with the crushed velvet and purple silk

of a blissful time

but how many more long nights and unfinished

goodbyes

how many more kisses in the dark and crying out of

sight

of a world that demands more than i can give

i want to drown in love but i am asked to live

a dual life, a could have been , an incomplete book of
poetry
i am asked to be me
all i want to be is yours. enslaved. urgent.
and free.

MERCURY

You try to hold on. But the water runs into the lines on your palm, soaking through, making your hand so heavy you cannot write a farewell note. An apology. An explanation.

You try again. But the sand coats your nails in a trance and you leave moon dust wherever you set off on your happy trails. The woods shimmer with light and the lotus pond is iridescent in places.

Something stronger you suggest to yourself. There's the breeze substantial with its host of secrets and bad dreams. It whips your hair around your face, a veil and you lose sight of forgiveness.

You keep trying. The light catches in your throat. Salt finds its way into your eyelashes and colours your view. Quicksilver is too steady to make quite the impact you're seeking.

You look in your straw bag for words you can use. Lack of substance, for want of another word, does not please you.

Finally, you use silence. A muteness that's deliberate and dangerous and insidious and unapologetic.

You realise, you need to explain yourself no longer and to no one.

DO FIERY FEMINISTS FALL IN LOVE?

I yearn for you. In every book and every song and every river and every dawn and every child and every sigh and every enemy and every smile and every walk and every cry and every prayer and every goodbye.

I yearn for you. In head bent against the cold breeze and rain, in sleet hammering at the windowpane, in silver blossoms cushioning my heavy footfall and in summer heat unkind to all.

I yearn for you. In every concert and play and at noon and yesterday and at repose and at running stance and at intermittent sleep and at elusive dance.

I yearn for you. In the space beneath my feet and in the hollow of my neck and in the back of my knee and in the temples grey hair deck and in the skin of my fingers and the gaps in my teeth and the barren womb inside me and in every odd heartbeat.

I yearn for you. In every argument and poem and tune and tone and empty words and terrible lines and purple prose and mood sublime and semi colon and comma and dash em en and over and letter and notebook and envelope and paper hook.

I yearn. But no, it's not really that bad.

EXILE

And when i emerged from the forest, nothing was the same. Friends were foes and foes were in the know. Uneasy alliances were easy and a different head wore the crown. Solitude has its gifts and its cost. It shows that love is earned not bought. It says that confrontation is good for the soul no matter what. It tells me i am hardly irreplaceable. It signifies that people will leave if they are able. So when i emerged from my cloud- filled retreat, full of zen and ideas about how to beat thoughts and feelings into submission, i found out then that i hadn't won. The thoughts remain, the lovers too, the weeds have grown and i outgrew my need to speak and to utter the words

i am all different or haven't you heard ?

NOVELTIES STORE

Don't bring your love to the bazaar
to sell amidst the tired coriander
and faded plastic
you want that someone see the miracle of your piety
but for pity's sake, the bazaar is not the place for it
don't bring your love to the *shandy*
surrounded by drunks high on arrack
and self-importance
bloated by mother blindness and wife impotence
stinking of fish and fumes and cheap perfume
what place your love here?
don't bring your love out
let it lie in the cupboard
among toe rings and property papers
and the origami he made for us
your love is a monument. a fossil. an anachronism.
it has no place in this world of polyamory and
priaps.
stop. with the trying and declaration of dying.
no one cares. not even, especially not, me.

MY KIND OF MATH

two hands but not mine

ten fingers but not yours

two tongues   you understand

legs entangled   how else can it be

twenty-four hundred strands of hair drape across
your chest

fingers try to forget themselves in me

breaths toomany   toofast to count

dreams are discrete and differential

emotions are tangential   even a null equation

the unknowns play algebra in the heart

sometimes math can be magical.

VIGIL

May you be the one to wait

At the gate

With an unlit lantern

Searching for the light of love-dim eyes.

Because even that may sometimes suffice

To bring relief to a love-drunk heart

That has mastered the art

Of outward indifference and inner war.

ONE-NIGHT STAND

I carry bites from bed to bed

Even the names a blur in my head

Am I with him or you today

Sometimes even I cannot say

All I know is how below me feels

He has a broad bed, more than king-size

His is a mat on the floor, fragrant with spice

And then there's the water bed not as fun as you

might think

This man doesn't care, all he wants is to drink

Me in

The beds are different the men are too

I look in all the faces and do not find you

Is that why I am on this journey

From bed to bed

To remember to renew to completely forget

It's hard to tell from where I am right now

The ceiling is painted his mouth a maw

He's moving the right way

And then he is not

This is ill-gotten gain

Given, not sought

No scratch that. I did seek it.

My own piece of meat. My own make it fit

My own piece of heaven. So fine, I wanted more

Three four five—I have stopped keeping score

Bed to bed is a journey

And it feels good.

It feels sinful too

Like all good love should.

SELF-PORTRAIT

back broken

straight mouthed

avid greyed

inches gained

pain jointed

pills popped

eyes maddened

grief bludgeoned

heart pummelled

spirit crushed

self destroyed

insanity belonged.

(me. after you.)

PAMUK PLAYS THE *PALLANGUZHI*

I talk to him about Vijay Nambisan. Reclusive poet.
Older brother.

He says there are many like him in his state.

Ayyappan died on the streets. Chullikkad is a warrior.
And MT is the greatest of them all.

"You English literature convent-educated girls—step
outside and look at the world."

My 'convent' was a government school with a ghost
in the bathroom.

The marble floors were broken cement and cobwebs
made for great hair ornaments.

It was first come first serve and the days you were
delayed, you squinted at the board in a dimly-lit
space, wondering about arithmetic.

No one taught me poetry then. It was Mr. Bell and
Mrs. Bell. It was Kutchu and his glasses.

English literature was a father's well-annotated
Shakespeare. It was *Murder in the Cathedral* and
Gitanjali. It was the state prayer, the few words of
Tamil I could only hum to.

I know not of Bharati, the man I share a birthday
with. I know not of Sangam poetry. I immerse
myself in the wine of *Madhushala* and look for the
saki. I sense the birth pangs in *Tamas* and read read
read.

Yes, I'm not partial to your tongue.

But I can quote Umberto and Wislawa, Neruda and
Saadat.

Life doesn't come in one dialect. Neither does love.

Neither does learning.

Neither does hubris.

Poets live and poets die, penniless

in any language.

Pallanguzhi: ancient Tamil manacle game

RECLAIMED LAND

The first thing I did when you left me for good, was to cut my hair. No. Not the one everyone sees. The one they don't. The one you love. I hated the way a thick bush made me feel. Itchy and swollen. You loved it. You loved the smell of it and the taste of it and the way your fingers got lost in it and the way, when you were done, it clung on to the white like it was home.

I cut it off. Short. Trim. Not enough to grab. Not enough to hold. Not enough to tickle your nose.

I didn't cut it all off. I'm a woman, not a little girl and the hair is mine. Just enough to feel protected.

I gave away all the clothes you liked. All those skirts that ended at the crotch. All those sleeveless blouses and chiffon saris. All those revealing tops that clung to my giant ass and showed everyone what you loved.

You loved me on display. You loved it when a man put an unwelcome arm around my waist. When a man stripped me with his eyes. I loved your pride. I called it love.

I moved back to my high-collared full sleeves dark black like the night outfits. I covered myself up with cotton stoles and north-eastern shawls and loose clothes. I girded my loins in every way and felt more me.

I swapped my whore red lipstick for something light. Strawberry margarita lip gloss. A hint of the shape you so loved to kiss. But now I claim it all.

This is my body.

These are my lips.

This is my cunt.

This is my heart.

This is my writing.

This is my life.

These are my people.

And you are nothing.

QUOTIDIAN

every few days i tell you

turn me over

cover me up

share

this bed filled with pillows and sheets

is bare

devoid of desire and the need to devour

each other

every few days you buy flowers

talk to the plants

look at me like a prized pet

not turn away when i walk around naked

every single day we wait for something

to give

to grow

to become intolerable.

every day is like every other day.

CALAVERA

New love is sitting at the table next to me holding
hands heads so close even silk wouldn't fit.

Old love is looking at the newspaper and reading a
book and not speaking at all.

New love is sharing soup and feeding croutons. It is
gazing with utter fascination and a smile that's
tantalising and distant as it listens to theories on
astronomy.

New love is right now holding a hand over a fist as it
pays the bill and doesn't wait for change.

Old love wonders about the tip.

New love is on the bike next to me. It's holding him
so close that rain water pools at the breasts and flows
along the sides of her body.

It's being gently caressed with every bump and every
stop and its thighs are jelly.

Old love is comfortably seated with a large bag in
between as it wonders about the couple next to it
and how that must feel.

New love doesn't need a raincoat an umbrella a jacket. It needs a warm palm against the chest and is electrified.

Old love is a pair of thick socks, an old t-shirt, a worn at the seat and knees corduroy that clings and comforts.

New love is a mint condition molecular gastronomy gif.

New love has dropped the napkin on the floor and is oblivious.

Old love is writing this poem.

Calavera: Artistic representation of the human skull. Usually made from sugar or clay, it is mostly associated with the Mexican celebration of the Day of the Dead or *Día de Muertos*.

SUNDER

it was easy before.

say goodbye. walk out the door. take your clothes
before you go.

those toilet seat shades. and those horrendous plaids.

the long collared shirts and the polka - dotted skirts.

it all fit in the Aristocrat. and that was that.

you ignored him outside movie halls. you did not
answer the odd phone call. you didn't go to reunion
trips.

you lost yourself in smoke haze sips and someone's
hips.

maybe he waited for an onionskin letter.

maybe he felt this was much better.

he stared at the old rotary and willed it to ring.

maybe nothing except the gas rings began to sing.

it was easier then. yes it was.

now there's no time to pause. there's so much to do
when love dies.

photos to delete. numbers to block.

status to change. man hours to clock.

things were simple then. sorrow too.

now the whole world knows about me. and about

you.

TINDER

The warm weight of a worried wondering heart rests lightly on the deep darkness of the night.

There is a voice calling and writing and pleading and guilting me into action and inaction to leavestay.

To listen to just be to say it will be okay.

That heart, the restless heart that leaves my bed with frequency mid-kiss mid-caress to stare at the moon or sing a tune that's only for one and cannot be played on a jukebox, that heart that wanders and will not be tied down because to be loved is to be tied down, that heart that walks away with no second glance and not a tear shed in regret or reproach or resignation.

That bastard heart now comes seeking me out like I am its salvation.

Across the bridge of distrust as recriminations stands this heart. It's come back, traipsing its way through explosive fury and loud sobbing fits. It looks at me voiceless, hoarse-throated from all the appeals for mercy.

You reject my one non- negotiable. And yet stand there lustful for the pleasures that only my being can provide.

I look across this vast abyss. My eyes cold my heart colder and my soul not in the mood for negotiation.

I light a match to your love letters. And set the whole damn place on fire.

AUTHAGRAPH

You know fifteen of the forty-eight moles that map my body.

You know the folds at my waist. The arch of my feet. And my toe rings.

You are aware of every breath I take when we are together.

You sense a change, even the slightest.

And can perhaps smell the desire I feel in my skin.

My body carries a perfume that only you know of. And that exists only for you.

Your tongue knows of the deep shadow of my navel. You have tasted wine and chocolate and salt there.

My arms have held you as you shuddered above me. You've felt their softness and their strength.

You know my hair and my ears and my nose.

You say that you see yourself in my eyes. Your mother in my eyes. Home in my eyes.

My lips are magic to you and you cannot stop marvelling at their shape their taste their touch.

You know every hair. You know the taste the clings to them earthy and musky and strong.

Your fingers have traced my insides.

Left their mark in the very marrow of my bones. Your body knows the heat of mine.

Does it know my heart?

AuthaGraph: An approximately equal-area world map projection invented by Japanese architect Hajime Narukawa in 1999.

MOTHER KNOWS BEST

tick bang ! bang! tock

goes my last legs biological clock

i am mammalian

oviparous but nulliparous

yeah those are big words and i know them.

i know what i am not.

not-mother.

so what does one wish a not-mother ?

what blessings are sought by a not-mother

who doesn't seem to be bothered

about being childless ?

a not-mother.

let's tell her:

may you grow more selfless

may you consider your parents

may you think of society and people and unknowns

and strangers and job seekers- who ask you why you

have no children—and other barren women who

wonder why they are cursed

for not being a mother is to be cursed

for what are your eggs if not be fused with other life-
creating goo

for what is a marriage if not to make three or four or
five from two

oh you poor not-mother woman

be less selfish

be more responsible

life isn't about having fun

life is about duty and fulfilling destiny.

but all they say, openly , to my face , is god bless you.

do well. best wishes. get healthy

where they mean

god bless you with children

do well and have a child

best wishes for a baby

get healthy so you can have a child

and the questions continue. and the speculation.

and then they ask the thing that scares me the most -

if you don't have children, who will you leave all your
books to?

HIRAETH

One night we are sitting at dinner. The table is plain. The crockery is white. The glasses are burgundy, the water is drunk. Over a frugal meal of rice and lentils, he tells me the same old story of lush rice fields and his mother's eyes. We sleep satiated, in more than one way.

The next morning, my hand reaches across the cheesecloth sheet and clutches air. He is gone. And I am alone. All day I wander in the garden where the bees are drunk on promise and the flowers blush with possessiveness. I talk to your beloved roses, but they are aware that I do not care too much for them, not like you do. I am the only woman whom you will allow the roses to adorn. Wrapped in my hair, spread on the bed, sprinkled on my pathway.

The ducks come looking for you, missing your shouts and hearty hey-hos. The cat wanders by and climbs into my ample lap, preferring my flesh to your bones. The dog is faithful as always but I can tell, he wonders about you.

At night, I set out a single placemat. It's made out of rushes and is yellow and brown. I use my fancy china, the one you find pretentious. And my glass has rosé. I can't bear rice. It is stone fruit and chocolate and rose cookies. I have the radio on. Around me the darkness is a breathing person.

I shall do this every day, and one day, my fingers will reach out and there you will be with your repentant mouth and sad eyes. We will go back to the before roles.

Till the next time. Till the next time my love, when the world and I are too much for your solitude.

Hiraeth: A longing for a 'home' you can't return to, or one that was never yours.

MOUNTAIN PASS

everywhere i went, you haunted me and now among the many shades of green, finally i am free.

Of your ghost and your need. This is how it comes to pass in bright autumnal colours and with the majesty of a many-tongued waterfall. It disappears in the oppressive crush of people who follow nothing except their own hearts. Their hearts cause traffic jams and irate passengers and create a mood that does not bode well for a mending. So amidst the generous display of what the world had to offer in green and greed in people and plants in water and wanderers, i let go of you. Wander my restless heart, breathe deep of the raw fragrance that punctuates the air like an exuberant exclamation point.

Search for your own self and soul and when you know, just let go.

DECLIVITY

The ice is melted. The conifers are bare. There's no air. Here.

The rocks are slippery. The road is uphill. There is no air here. Still.

The water is muddy. The fish all dead. There is no air here. Moss fed.

The house is dusty. The books are gone. There is no air here. Torn.

This love story is lost. The lucre of stars and gold. There is no air here. All told.

SMOKESCREEN

An intolerance to ambiguity means that i search for
you in places you told me you wouldn't be.
In books and buses.
Roads and rogues.
In the decadent disarray of bedsheets in black and
white.
You said you wouldn't appear but there i am at the
stoop, holding an ineffectual and curious broom to
give my vigil, legitimacy.
i search for you in the placid waters of life passing
me by, wondering why i don't see the need to go
along for the ride.
i look for you in tea-gardens and ceremonies, coffee
pots and dregs, that stiff glass of whisky and in every
word i read.
Yes this need to find is a recurrent theme in my life.
And the need for ambiguity and locating the swiftest
exit is yours.
So i look for entrances and exits too, block them
with sheer force of will and wishful thinking and find
myself puzzled when neither is enough.

An intolerance to ambiguity means i do not like unfinished business. Loose ends and strings that toss about in the breeze, so ineffectual, but that weigh me down like an anchor.

Mountains, streams and seas.

Flowers, birds and trees.

i look for you in constellations and condiments.

In silver sands and the fragrance of woodsmoke.

i look for you in termite hills and old sofas.

You're good at camouflage.

But it's early days yet.

And i can always intensify my search.

FINDING YOURSELF

It's just a poem

A poem to write in those many hours

Of waiting for you.

Don't read too much into it.

The man could be you or anyone.

The woman is me or anyone else.

The dreams are mine or nightmares.

The want real or fake.

It's hard to say when a poet is lying.

It's not clear-cut like real life and it's not like ordinary

people.

Poets blend life and love and longing and lying so

well, even they don't always know what's what.

How then, would you?

A child is not a child. It's a book.

A life is not a life. It's an escape.

Someone else is not someone else. It's revenge.

You'd be mistaken

if you said this poem here is for you.

If you said there look that's about my hands and my

lips and my lovemaking.

It could be you. It could be him. It could be anyone.

Read a poem. Let it speak to you.

And then let it be.